Meal Prep
Made it Easy!

Meal Prepping for Beginners with Healthy Recipes for Weight Loss

---

Emma Green

Disclaimer

The recipes and information in this book are provided for educational purposes only. Please always consult a licensed professional before making changes to your lifestyle or diet. The author and/or publisher shall have neither liability nor responsibility to anyone with respect to any loss or damage caused or alleged to be caused directly or indirectly by the information contained in this book. All trademarks and brands within this book are for clarifying purposes only and are owned by the owners themselves, not affiliated with this document.

Images from shutterstock.com

CONTENTS

INTRODUCTION

Happiness is a meal-prepped fridge.

Freezing is the best conservation method ever invented by mother nature herself. Just think of it—in winter, all plants freeze, their roots, bulbs, seeds, everything freezes. But they not only do not die, they start growing and blooming in spring. To save live plants, nature, unlike the human beings, doesn't boil, pickle or smoke. Nature freezes!

Freezer meals have saved thousands of working housewives, newbie mothers, and just about everyone dreading the dinner hour. The moto of freezing is, "Cook once, eat the whole week/month." If you can plan out a few meals ahead of time, you feel much more organized. If you have the freezer full of ready-made breakfasts for the whole week, you feel like a relieved superhero.

Every dish in this book is freezable with no harm to its taste. You will find a wide variety of casserole recipes for dinner and breakfast. What could be easier than tossing together protein, carbs, and veggies into one dish?

You will find recipes for stocks, patties, marinades, and much more.

Freezing Rules

The principles of successful and healthy freezing include:

- Always cool food before freezing
- Use BPA free containers
- Freeze food in portions so that you don't defrost the whole pan to feed 1 person
- Labels with the date
- Never refreeze raw food
- To prevent ice chunks, freeze for couple hours first and only then freeze for long in individual containers
- When freezing fresh whole berries, place them on a cutting board or tray so that they do not touch each other and freeze slightly. Only then fill the bags. Then the berries don't get in one big lump and will be stored safe and intact.
- The temperature in the freezer must be no less than minus 18°C or -0.4°F.
- Sort foods by their type and divide between the drawers. Products can soak in foreign smells, so don't keep fish, strawberrries, or mushrooms in same drawer.

Temperature Danger Zone

THE DANGER ZONE

- 60-140 DEGREES*
  - Bacteria produce quickly in the presence of food, moisture, and warmth (including room temperature). Food poisoning bacteria thrive at room temperature!
  - Hot foods should not be held below 140 degrees.
- 160-212 DEGREES
  - High temperatures kill most harmful bacteria.
- 40 DEGREES & BELOW
  - Cold temperatures slow down the growth of bacteria.
- 0 DEGREES (FREEZING)
  - Bacteria stops growing.

Foods That Don't Freeze Well

As you may know, freezing changes the texture of food as it's thawed; that is why it is not a good idea to freeze all food. Some foods may turn mushy or watery when thawed. Products that don't freeze well include:

- vegetables with high moisture content (change in consistency)
- fresh onions (change in taste)
- boiled potatoes (will darken)
- hard cheese (crumbles into small pieces after thawing)
- eggs in shell (shell may crack)
- ready made cold salads
- cultured milk foods (may clot)
- egg and flour based sauces (change in consistency)

Also remember that repeated freezing may be not healthy. When you get the food out of the freezer, some bacteria reactivate while thawing. If you put the food back in the freezer again, these bacteria not only survive but thrive. Although boiling the thawed product first won't harm it if frozen for a second time.

Containers to Use

You will require:

- Containers with covers
- Ziploc bags
- Small jars
- Food wrap
- Foil

You want containers that are:

- BPA free
- Freezer safe
- Microwavable
- Stackable
- Reusable

→ HOW LONG CAN YOU ←
KEEP FOOD
IN THE FREEZER?

 **WHOLE CHICKEN**
1 YEAR

 **BEEF ROASTS**
6 MONTHS

 **CHICKEN PIECES**
9 MONTHS

 FRUITS AND VEGGIES
1 MONTH

 **SALMON**
3 MONTHS

 **NUTS**
6 MONTHS

 **COD OR FLOUNDER**
6 MONTHS

 **BREAD**
1 MONTH

 **GROUND BEEF, LAMB OR PORK**
3 MONTHS

 **SOUP**
2 MONTHS

 **PORK CHOPS OR LAMB CHOPS**
6 MONTHS

 **CASSEROLES**
2 MONTHS

 **STEAK**
6 MONTHS

Breakfast

Pancake Batter

Prep time: 15 minutes

Cooking time:1 hour

Servings: 50 pancakes

Nutrients (per 5 cups batter):

Total Carbs – 215 g

Fat – 52.5 g

Protein – 61 g

Calories – 1641

Ingredients:

- 2 large eggs
- 2 cups milk, warm
- 2 cups water, warm
- 2 Tbsp sugar
- 2 Tbsp oil
- 2 cups flour or more if needed
- Pinch of salt

Instructions:

1. In a large bowl, beat the eggs. Add milk and water a ½ cup at a time, constantly whisking.
2. Add sugar and salt, whisk well.
3. Gradually add flour, constantly whisking until the batter is thick enough to pour easily.
4. Add oil and stir.
5. Divide the batter between ziplock bags and freeze. Can be stored up to 3 months at.

Pancake Egg Filling

Prep time: 5 minutes

Cooking time: 10 min

Servings: 10

Nutrients per serving:

Total Carbs – 0.6 g

Fat – 1.9 g

Protein – 2.6 g

Calories – 31

Ingredients:

- 4 hard boiled eggs
- ½ cup spring onions, chopped
- 2 Tbsp fresh dill, minced
- Pinch of salt

Instructions:

1. Dice the egg.
2. Combine all ingridients and season with salt.
3. Spoon some filling onto a pancake and roll.
4. Freeze the stuffed pancakes and warm in a preheated pan with some butter, covered.

Pancake Apple Walnuts Filling

Prep time: 5 minutes

Cooking time: 10 min

Servings: 10

Nutrients per serving:

Total Carbs – 6.6 g

Fat – 0.4 g

Protein – 0.1 g

Calories – 27

Ingredients:

- 2 sweet and sour apples, cored, grated
- 3 Tbsp walnuts, crushed
- 1 Tbsp raisins
- 1-2 Tbsp sugar
- Pinch of cinnamon

Instructions:

1. Combine all ingridients and spoon some filling onto a pancake and roll.
2. Freeze the stuffed pancakes and warm in a preheated pan with some butter, covered.

Pancake Mushroom Filling

Prep time: 15 minutes

Cooking time: 30 minutes

Servings: 10

Nutrients per serving:

Total Carbs – 3.8 g

Fat – 0.7 g

Protein – 4.6 g

Calories – 37

Ingredients:

- 18 oz Champignon mushrooms, chopped
- 1 chicken breast, boiled, shredded
- 2 onion, chopped
- Salt and pepper, to taste
- Sour cream for serving

Instructions:

1. In a preheated pan with some oil, sauté onions for 2-3 minutes, add mushrooms and season with salt and pepper. Cook for 15 minutes, add chicken and cook for 10 minutes more. Mix well.
2. Spoon some filling onto a pancake and roll.
3. Freeze the stuffed pancakes and warm in a preheated pan with some butter, covered.
4. Serve with sour cream.

Curd Fritters

Prep time: 15 minutes

Cooking time: 15 minutes

Servings: 6

Nutrients per serving:

Total Carbs – 37.5 g

Fat – 7.9 g

Protein – 85.8 g

Calories – 575

Ingredients:

- 35 oz cottage cheese
- 2 eggs
- 2 Tbsp sugar
- 1 Tbsp coconut flakes
- 1 cup flour

Instructions:

1. Combine cottage cheese, sugar, egggs, flour and mix well.
2. Shape into balls and press to make them flat.
3. Preheat oven to 392°F.
4. Arange the fritters onto a baking sheet and bake for 10 min. Flip, and cook on the other side for 5 min.
5. Let the curd fritters cool and arrange into a container, cover with a food wrap and freeze.
6. When serving, warm up in the oven or microwave.

Curd Snacks

Prep time: 15 minutes

Cooking time: 5 minutes

Servings: 6

Nutrients per serving:

Total Carbs – 23.4 g

Fat – 19.2 g

Protein – 13 g

Calories – 299

Ingredients:

- 2 cups cottage cheese
- 2/3 stick butter
- 2 Tbsp cacao powder
- 3 Tbsp sugar
- 4 Tbsp sour cream
- 3.5 oz crunchy cookies, crushed
- 5 lbs milk chocolate bar, melted

Instructions:

1. Blen together cottage cheese and sour cream.
2. Add sugar and whisk until smooth.
3. Add soft butter and whisk until smooth.
4. Add crushed cookies and cacao and whisk until smooth.
5. Cover a plate with food wrap and spoon out the snacks, making the desired shape.
6. To glaze the snacks, dip each piece in melted chocolate using two forks.
7. Let the chocolate thicken and wrap the curd snacks in foil.
8. Freeze.

Curd Pudding

Prep time: 40 minutes

Cooking time: 40 minutes

Servings: 6

Nutrients per serving:

Total Carbs – 29.3 g

Fat – 7.9 g

Protein – 12.6 g

Calories – 236

Ingredients:

- 2 cups cottage cheese
- ½ cup sugar
- ½ cup semolina
- 2 eggs
- 3-4 Tbsp milk
- ½ stick butter, softened

Instructions:

1. Combine all ingridients and add to a greased baking dish. Let stand for 40 minutes.
2. Bake at 392°F until golden – about 40 minutes.

Liver Pate

Prep time: 5 minutes

Cooking time: 15 minutes

Servings: 6

Nutrients per serving:

Total Carbs – 6.6 g

Fat – 30.2 g

Protein – 26.4 g

Calories – 401

Ingredients:

- 2 lbs chicken liver, rinsed, cut into pieces
- 2 carrots, chopped
- 2 onions,chopped
- ½ stick butter
- Salt and pepper, to taste

Instructions:

1. In a preheated pan with some oil, add liver and cook over high heat until lightly brown.
2. Add onions and carrots. Cook until the liver is soft and juicy.
3. Let cool. Pass trough mincing machine and add butter. Season with salt and pepper. Blend with a blender until smooth.
4. Transfer to containers and freeze.

Omelette mixture

Prep time: 15 minutes

Servings: 8

Nutrients per serving:

Total Carbs – 6.9 g

Fat – 0.2 g

Protein – 1.5 g

Calories – 31

Ingredients:

- 3 medium tomatoes, seeded, cubed
- 3 red bell peppers, seeded, cubed
- 3 spring onions, chopped
- ½ cup green peas

Instructions:

1. Place each vegetable into separate zip lock bags and freeze.
2. When the vegetables are a little icy, combine in 6 ziploc bag and freeze.
3. Use in omelettes or other dishes.

Apple Butter

Prep time: 15 minutes

Cooking time: 2 hours

Servings: 3-4 jars

Nutrients per 4 jars:

Total Carbs – 475 g

Fat – 0.7 g

Protein – 1.6 g

Calories – 1732

Ingredients:

- 4 lbs Granny Smith apples, quartered
- 1 cup apple cider vinegar
- 1/2 cup of sugar, for each cup of apple pulp
- 2 tsp cinnamon
- ½ tsp ground cloves
- ½ tsp allspice
- 1 lemon, juice and grated rind
- 2 cups water

Instructions:

1. Put the apples in a large pot. Add vinegar and water, cover, bring to a boil.
2. Let simmer until apples are soft, about 20 minutes.
3. Remove from heat and puree the apples using a food sieve or mill.
4. Add sugar, spices, lemon rind, and juice.
5. Put the apple mixture into a large pot and cook over medium heat, stirring until thickened, about 1 hour.
6. Pour into sterilized jars and freeze.

Mini Pizzas

Prep time: 15 min

Cooking time: 15 min

Servings: 4

Nutrients per serving:

Total Carbs – 19.2 g

Fat – 5.5 g

Protein – 12.6 g

Calories – 174

Ingredients:

- 4 slices toast bread, crust cut off
- 1 cup soft cheese, grated
- 1 cup ham, chopped
- 1 cup mushrooms, chopped
- ½ cup black olives, sliced
- 1 tomato, sliced
- 2 Tbsp ketchup

Instructions:

1. Spread ketchup over bread slice.
2. Add ham, mushrooms, olives, tomato slices and cheese.
3. Cover with food wrap and freeze.
4. When serving, let thaw for 10 minutes and bake in the oven at 400F for 15 minutes.

Oats Pecan Scones

Prep time: 15 minutes

Cooking time: 15 minutes

Servings: 4

Nutrients per serving:

Total Carbs – 87.3 g

Fat – 33 g

Protein – 16.6 g

Calories – 682

Ingredients:

- 1 cup oats, grinded
- 1 1/2 cups flour
- 2 Tbsp sugar
- 1 egg
- 1 Tbsp baking powder
- 4 Tbsp maple syrup
- 2 1/2 Tbsp butter, cut into small pieces
- 1/2 cup Half and Half
- 1/2 cup chopped pecans

Instructions:

1. Mix together flour, oats, sugar, salt, and baking powder. Add maple syrup and butter.
2. In a separate bowl, beat together eggs and Half and Half.
3. Combine the two mixtures.
4. Add in the chopped pecans and mix well.
5. Form equal sized balls.
6. Place on a baking sheet and flatten the balls. Bake for 15 minutes.
7. Serve and freeze the rest.

Oatmeal Cups

Prep time: 15 minutes

Cooking time: 3 min

Servings: 4

Nutrients per serving:

Total Carbs – 93.6 g

Fat – 11.8 g

Protein – 25.9 g

Calories – 573

Ingredients:

- 3 cups oats
- 2 tsp honey
- 3 cups water
- 3 cups milk
- Toppings of your liking – nuts, raisins, fruits

Instructions:

1. Combine milk and water in a pot. Add oats and honey.
2. Bring to boil, reduce heat & cook for 3 minutes, stirring.
3. Grease muffin tin with cooking spray.
4. Divide the oats between the cups and top with desired topping.
5. To freeze, cover and place in the freezer. Once frozen, transfer to a bag.
6. To cook, transfer the desired number of cups to a fridge overnight and microwave in the morning.

Vegetable Muffins

Prep time: 15 minutes

Cooking time: 40 minutes

Servings: 4

Nutrients per serving:

Total Carbs – 11.5 g

Fat – 8.4 g

Protein – 12.9 g

Calories – 166

Ingredients:

- 1 zucchini squash, peeled, grated
- 2 carrots, cut in small cubes
- 2 onions, cut in small cubes
- ½ lb ground chicken
- 1 egg
- 1 bunch parsley, minced
- 1 bunch dill, minced
- 1 Tbsp olive oil
- Salt and pepper, to taste

Instructions:

1. In a skillet, sauté onions and carrots using olive oil until golden.
2. In a bowl, combine ground chicken, grated squash, onions, carrots, greens. Add egg and season with salt and pepper.
3. Grease muffin tin with cooking spray.
4. Fill the tins with chicken vegetable mixture.
5. Bake at 392°F for 30—40 minutes.
6. Freeze when cooled. When serving microwave or heat up in the oven.

Carrot Pancakes

Prep time: 5 minutes

Cooking time: 20 minutes

Servings: 8

Nutrients per serving:

Total Carbs– 4.9 g

Fat – 0.5 g

Protein – 1.2 g

Calories – 27

Ingredients:

- 6 large carrots, peeled, grated
- 1 large egg
- 2 Tbsp almond flour
- 1 Tbsp parsley
- 1 Tbsp thyme
- 1 tsp mustard
- Salt and pepper, to taste

Instructions:

1. Mix all ingredients with a fork and make small patties.
2. To freeze, place raw patties on a parchment paper or lined tray and freeze until hard. Then transfer to bags for longer storage.
3. When ready to cook, place on a baking sheet lined with parchment paper and bake in a preheated 375°F oven for 20 minutes.

Burgundian Apple Flan

Prep time: 15 minutes

Cooking time: 35 minutes

Servings: 4

Nutrients per serving:

Total Carbs – 38 g

Fat – 12.2 g

Protein – 3.7 g

Calories – 264

Ingredients:

- 4 apples, peeled, cored, cubed
- 2 eggs
- ½ stick butter
- ½ cup milk
- 3 Tbsp flour
- 6 Tbsp icing sugar
- 2 dashes cinnamon

Instructions:

1. Melt some butter in a pot and add the apples. Let stew for 2-3 minutes.
2. Sieve flour into a shallow bowl, add icing sugar and eggs. Mix well.
3. Add apples into the batter and stir.
4. Grease a baking dish with butter.
5. Pour the flan mixture into the baking dish and sprinkle with cinnamon.
6. Bake for 35 minutes at 356°F.
7. Freeze when cooled in a plastic container.

Very Berrie Smoothie

Prep time: 15 minutes

Cooking time: 2 minutes

Servings: 6

Nutrients per serving:

Total Carbs – 19.8 g

Fat – 2.3 g

Protein – 3.9 g

Calories – 106

Ingredients:

- 2 cups blueberries
- 2 cups strawberries
- 2 cups raspberries
- 2 cups milk/almond milk
- ½ cup apple juice

Instructions:

1. Combine all ingridients in a blender and blend until smooth.
2. Take non shouldered jars (16 oz is good enough for 1 portion).
3. Fill the jars, leaving 2-3 inches at the top, and put into the freezer.
4. If you want your smooothie for breakfast transfer the jar to the refrigerator to thaw overnight.

Lunch

Greek Stuffed Peppers

Prep time: 15 minutes

Cooking time: 45 minutes

Servings: 10

Nutrients per serving:

Total Carbs – 14.8 g

Fat – 11.9 g

Protein – 7.5 g

Calories – 188

Ingredients:

- 10 bell peppers,seeded, tops removed
- 3 tomatoes, cubed finely
- 1 onion, chopped finely
- 2 spring onions, chopped finely
- 1 garlic clove, minced
- 2 Tbsp olive oil
- 1 cup rice, rinsed
- 3 Tbps soy sauce
- ½ cup chopped almonds
- 3 cups Brinsen cheese, cubed
- 1 1/2 cups water
- Salt and pepper, to taste

Instructions:

1. In a pan with olive oil, saute garlic, onions, and 1 spring onion for 3-4 minutes, stirring.
2. Add tomatoes and cook for 3 minutes more.
3. Add soy sauce and rice. Pour in water. Cook for 15 minutes, covered.
4. When the rice is ready, let the mixture cool and then add the cheese, almonds, and remaining spring onions.
5. Season with salt and pepper, to taste.
6. Stuff the peppers with the filling and place into containers. Freeze.
7. To cook the peppers, put them into a baking dish with some water and bake in 392°F oven for 45 minutes.

Beef & Pork Patties

Prep time: 15 minutes

Cooking time: 45 minutes

Servings: 8

Nutrients per serving:

Total Carbs – 6.4 g

Fat – 59.6 g

Protein – 84.8 g

Calories – 925

Ingredients:

- 14 oz ground beef
- 14 oz ground pork
- 2 onion, chopped
- 4 Tbsp semolina
- Salt and pepper, to taste

Instructions:

1. Combine all ingridients, then shape into patties.
2. Put into the freezer for a couple of hours, then transfer to a ziploc bag or any container.
3. To cook the patties, preheat a pan with some oil and cook on both sides for about 5 min on each side.

Oats and Pork Patties

Prep time: 15 minutes

Cooking time: 45 minutes

Servings: 6

Nutrients per serving:

Total Carbs – 8.9 g

Fat – 32 g

Protein – 41.8 g

Calories – 501

Ingredients:

- 2 lbs ground pork
- 5 Tbsp oats, fine ground
- 2 onions, processed in blender
- 2 eggs
- Salt and pepper, to taste

Instructions:

1. Combine onions, eggs, and ground pork, season with salt and pepper.
2. Add oats and mix until smooth.
3. Form patties and put on a cutting board lined with food wrap.
4. Place the patties in the freezer for a couple of hours, then take them out and transfer to a labeled container.
5. Cook the patties in the oven at 350°F for 40 minutes.

Fish Patties

Prep time: 15 minutes

Cooking time: 45 minutes

Servings: 6

Nutrients per serving:

Total Carbs – 8.3 g

Fat – 1.5 g

Protein – 49.7 g

Calories – 254

Ingredients:

- 3 lbs fresh water fish fillets
- 2 onions, chopped
- 1 egg
- 1 Tbsp semolina
- Salt and pepper, to taste
- Pinch of fish seasoning
- ½ cup Breadcrumbs

Instructions:

1. Mince fish fillets.
2. Add the egg, onions, and semolina to the ground fish. Season with salt, pepper, and fish seasoning.
3. Let stand for 20 minutes.
4. Form patties and coat in breadcrumbs.
5. To freeze, place patties on a board lined with parchment paper and freeze until hard. Then transfer to bags for longer storage.
6. To prepare fish patties, fry in a preheated pan with olive oil for about 5 min on each side.

Sesame Crusted Cutlets

Prep time: 15 minutes

Cooking time: 8 minutes

Servings: 4

Nutrients per serving:

Total Carbs – 51 g

Fat – 14.3 g

Protein – 33.4 g

Calories – 469

Ingredients:

- 4 boneless pork chops
- 2 eggs
- 1 1/2 cups breadcrumbs
- ½ cup sesame seeds
- Salt and pepper to taste

Instructions:

1. Pound the chops with a meat malllet to about 1 1/2" thick.
2. Prepare the coating by whisking eggs in one bowl and together breadcrumbs and sesame seeds in another bowl.
3. Dip each cutlet into the egg mixture and then into the sesame mixture.
4. Bake the cutlets in a skillet with some olive oil and cook at 482°F for 4 minutes on each side or until golden.

5. Let the cutlets cool, freeze for a couple hours on a board, not touching each other, then transfer to a bag.
6. To serve heat up in the oven and serve with spinach.

Potato patties

Prep time: 20 minutes

Cooking time: 20 minutes

Servings: 4

Nutrients per serving:

Total Carbs – 22 g

Fat – 0.9 g

Protein – 3.7 g

Calories – 303

Ingredients:

- 2 big potatoes, peeled, boiled, grated
- 1 egg
- Flour for dredging
- Sour cream for serving
- Fresh dill for serving

Instructions:

1. Add an egg to the grated potatoes and form the patties.
2. To freeze, place raw patties on a board lined with parchment paper and freeze until hard. Then transfer to bags for longer storage.
3. Preheat the oven to 400°F and lay the patties onto a baking sheet sprayed with nonstick spray.
4. Cook for 20 minutes or until golden, turning several times.
5. Serve with sour cream and fresh dill.

Cold Tomato Soup

Prep time: 15 minutes

Cooking time: 30 minutes

Servings: 2 bags (2 gal)

Nutrients per 2 bags:

Total Carbs – 13.5 g

Fat – 22.8 g

Protein – 4 g

Calories – 288

Ingredients:

- 13 cups fresh tomatoes, chopped
- 5 garlic cloves, minced
- 3 Tbsp olive oil
- 2 cups chicken stock
- 2 cups heavy whipping cream
- Fresh basil
- 2 dashes celery salt
- Salt and pepper, to taste

Instructions:

1. In a skillet, sauté garlic using olive oil. Season with salt and pepper.
2. Add in chopped tomatoes and let simmer for 15 minutes.
3. Pour in 2 cups stock, stir and let cool.
4. Transfer to a blender and blend until smooth.
5. Split soup into 2 ziploc bags and freeze.
6. When preparing, thaw and reheat tomato base and add in cream.
7. Serve with fresh basil.

Chicken Stock

Prep time: 15 minutes

Cooking time: 3 hours

Servings: 4 cups

Nutrients per 4 cups:

Total Carbs – 32.8 g

Fat – 8 g

Protein – 23 g

Calories – 310

Ingredients:

- 1 chicken carcass, broken into pieces
- 2 onions, peeled, whole
- 2 carrots, peeled, cut into chunks
- 2 celery stalks, chopped
- 2 bay leaves
- 1 tsp thyme
- 1 tsp sage
- Salt and pepper to taste
- 4 cups water

Instructions:

1. In a pot, cover the chicken pieces with water. Add the whole onions.
2. Bring to boil, then let simmer over low heat for 30 minutes.
3. Add carrots and spices. Let simmer for 2 hours. Add water if needed.
4. Strain the broth and freeze in ziploc bags.

Meat Baskets

Prep time: 15 minutes

Cooking time: 45 minutes

Servings: 2

Nutrients per serving:

Total Carbs – 16.5 g

Fat – 15.9 g

Protein – 31.5 g

Calories – 324

Ingredients:

- 2 pork chops
- 1 carrot, chopped
- 1 leek, chopped
- 1 zucchini, chopped
- 1-2 sweet peppers, chopped
- 4 Tbsp hard cheese, grated
- Salt and pepper, to taste

Instructions:

1. Pound the chops with a meat malllet to about 1 1/2" thick and season with salt and pepper.
2. In a bowl, mix the vegetables together.
3. Place the vegetables on the pork chops.
4. Wrap in foil and put into a preheated 390°F oven.
5. After 30 minutes, take out and sprinkle with cheese and bake for 10 minutes more.
6. Serve immediately or freeze in foil when cooled.

Stuffed Cabbage Rolls

Prep time: 30 minutes

Cooking time: 45 minutes

Servings: 6

Nutrients per serving:

Total Carbs – 17.8 g

Fat – 5.6 g

Protein – 23.6 g

Calories – 214

Ingredients:

- 1 head cabbage
- 15 oz ground meat (beef+pork)
- ½ cup rice, half cooked
- 1 onion, chopped
- 1 carrot, grated
- Small buch parsley, minced
- Small bunch dill, minced
- Salt and pepper, to taste
- 1-2 cups tomato juice for stewing

Instructions:

1. Boil cabbage in salted water and remove the cabbage leaves.
2. In a frying pan, cook the onions and grated carrots using some olive oil.
3. Combine rice, ground meat, onions, and carrots. Season with salt and pepper, add minced parsley and dill and mix well.
4. Spoon some filling on a cabbage leaf and roll.
5. Freeze.
6. When preparing, let stew in tomato juice.

Lazy Cabbage Rolls

Prep time: 30 minutes

Cooking time: 1 hour 20 minutes

Servings: 6

Nutrients per serving:

Total Carbs – 10.6 g

Fat – 10.3 g

Protein – 15.3 g

Calories – 192

Ingredients:

- ½ lb cabbage, shredded
- 1 lb ground chicken
- 1 onion, chopped
- Salt and pepper, to taste
- ½ cup Breadcrumbs
- ½ cup sour cream
- 2 Tbsp tomato paste
- ½ cup Water

Instructions:

1. Combine ground chicken, cabbage, and onions. Season with salt and pepper.
2. Form patties and coat them in bread crumbs.
3. Let freeze on a board for a couple hours, then transfer to bags in portions.
4. To cook, bake them in the oven at 400F for 20 minutes.
5. In a bowl, mix sour cream, tomato paste, and water.
6. Transfer the patties to a pot and add sauce. Let simmer over low for an hour.

White Bean Stuffed Bell Peppers

Prep time: 20 minutes

Cooking time: 45 minutes

Servings: 6

Nutrients per serving:

Total Carbs – 36.5 g

Fat – 10.5 g

Protein – 24.8 g

Calories – 338

Ingredients:

- 6 bell peppers, tops and seeds removed, rinsed
- 1 lb turkey breast
- 1 cup cooked rice
- 1 onion, diced
- 6 garlic cloves, quartered
- 1 15-oz can white beans
- 1 1/2 cups tomato sauce
- 4 oz Mozarella
- ½ cup basil, chopped
- 2 tsp olive oil
- 1 Tbsp Italian seasoning
- 1 Tbsp oregano
- Salt and pepper to taste

Instructions:

1. Using a blender, blend together 1 ¼ cup tomato sauce, garlic and basil.

2. In a skillet, sauté the onion using olive oil. Add turkey, grounding the meat. Cook until meat is no longer pink.
3. Stir in sauce from the blender. Season with oregano and Italian herbs. Let simmer for 10 minutes.
4. Stir in beans and rice. Season with salt and pepper.
5. Place bell peppers into a baking dish and fill the peppers with turkey mixture. Top with tomato sauce and Mozarella.
6. Freeze in plastic containers.
7. When cooking cover with foil and bake at 350°F for 30-45 minutes.

Chicken Nuggets

Prep time: 10 minutes

Cooking time: 20 minutes

Servings: 6

Nutrients per serving:

Total Carbs – 33.5 g

Fat – 11 g

Protein – 24.6 g

Calories – 324

Ingredients:

- 1 ½ lbs chicken fillet, cut into nuggets size
- 5 eggs
- 1 cup flour
- 1 cup cornflake crumbs
- 1 Tbsp paprika flakes
- Salt and pepper, to taste

Instructions:

1. Combine flour, paprika, salt, and pepper.
2. Coat each chicken piece first in flour then in eggs and in cornflakes generously.
3. Place nuggets on a baking tray lined with parchment paper.
4. Bake at 356°F for 15-20 minutes.
5. Freeze nuggets when cooled.

Chicken Paella

Prep time: 20 minutes

Cooking time: 50 minutes

Servings: 8

Nutrients per serving:

Total Carbs – 33 g

Fat – 5 g

Protein – 7 g

Calories – 370

Ingredients:

- 8 boneless, skinless chicken thighs, cut into chunks
- 2 onions, chopped
- 4 garlic cloves, crushed
- 3 cups paella rice
- 4 sweet peppers, deseeded, sliced
- 4 oz green beans, trimmed, blanched
- 6 ripe tomatoes, cut into chunks
- 2 Tbsp olive oil
- 8 1/2 cups chicken stock
- 1 Tbsp smoked sweet paprika
- Fresh parsley, chopped
- Salt and pepper, to taste

Instructions:

1. In a large skillet, brown the chicken using olive oil. Cook until golden and put aside.
2. Add onions to the pan & cook for 6 minutes, until soft.
3. Add garlic and paprika and cook for 1 minute.
4. Add rice and stir well.
5. Add the stock & let simmer for 10 minutes.
6. Return the chicken to the pan and add peppers, tomatoes, and beans. Season with salt and pepper.
7. Stir & cook for 5 minutes, or until the rice is tender and the liquid evaporates.
8. Top with fresh parsley and divide between freezer proof boxes.

Chicken Fried Rice

Prep time: 20 minutes

Cooking time: 50 minutes

Servings: 6

Nutrients per serving:

Total Carbs – 50 g

Fat – 5 g

Protein – 15 g

Calories – 309

Ingredients:

- 1 cup roast chicken, chopped
- 3 1/2 cups rice, uncooked
- 8 eggs
- 1 package frozen vegetable mix
- 1 package Fried Rice seasoning mix
- 1 tsp butter
- 2 tbsp Olive oil
- Salt and pepper, to taste

Instructions:

1. Cook the rice according.
2. Beat the eggs and season salt and pepper.
3. Scramble the eggs in a pan with 1 tsp of butter, and set aside.
4. Add ¼ cup oil to the pan and add the chopped chicken.

5. Add the vegetables and seasoning mix to the chicken. Cook until the vegetables are done.
6. Add in scrambled eggs.
7. Add the cooked rice and stir.
8. Transfer to ziploc bags to freeze.
9. To warm up, place the frozen fried rice in an oven safe dish and bake for 40 minutes at 350°F.

Sautéed Mushrooms

Prep time: 10 minutes

Cooking time: 20 minutes

Servings: 6

Nutrients per serving:

Total Carbs – 17 g

Fat – 7 g

Protein – 4 g

Calories – 130

Ingredients:

- 2 lbs Champignon mushrooms, rinsed, sliced
- 4 green onions, chopped
- 6 garlic cloves, minced
- ½ cup coconut oil
- 4 Tbsp butter
- 1/3 cup white wine
- 1 cup fresh parsley, chopped
- Salt and pepper, to taste

Instructions:

1. In a large skillet, sauté green onions using olive oil until tender.
2. Add the mushrooms and butter, season with salt and pepper. Stir well.
3. As soon as the butter melts add the wine and cook for 5 minutes.
4. Add minced garlic and cook for another 2 minutes.
5. Once the liquid has evaporated, remove from heat let cool, and freeze.

Chicken Spring Rolls in Jars

Prep time: 10 minutes

Cooking time: 15 minutes

Servings: 4

Nutrients per serving:

Total Carbs – 14 g

Fat – 4.8 g

Protein – 2.5 g

Calories – 110

Ingredients:

- 1 lb ground chicken
- 2 cups vermicelli noodles, cooked
- 1 cup red pepper, sliced
- 1 cup cucumber, cut into straws
- 2 garlic cloves, minced
- 1 Tbsp ginger, minced
- 2 Tbsp soy sauce
- 1 Tbsp sesame oil
- 1/3 cup cilantro, chopped
- ¼ cup sesame seeds
- ½ sweet chili sauce
- Salt and pepper, to taste

Instructions:

1. In a skillet, sauté ground chicken using sesame oil. Season with salt and pepper. Add soy sauce and cook for 2-3 minutes.
2. Add garlic and ginger, sauté until the chicken is fully cooked.
3. Take 4 jars and add sweet chili sauce. Divide chicken, cucumber and red pepper between the jars. Top with noodles, sesame seeds, and fresh cilantro.

Pasta Salad

Prep time: 15 minutes

Cooking time: 25 minutes

Servings: 4

Nutrients per serving:

Total Carbs – 35 g

Fat – 19 g

Protein – 32 g

Calories – 450

Ingredients:

- 2 cups uncooked pasta rotini
- 2 chicken breasts
- 1 Tbsp sesame oil
- 1 Tbsp soy sauce
- 2 tbsp Sesame seeds
- 10 oz Mann's Power Blend

For the vinaigrette:

- 2 Tbsp olive oil
- 2 Tbsp rice vinegar
- 1 1/2 Tbsp sesame oil
- 1 1/2 Tbsp honey
- ¾ tsp soy sauce

Instructions:

1. Cook the pasta according to directions.
2. In a bowl, mix sesame oil and soy sauce. Toss the chicken in mixture and bake at 425°F for 10 minutes on each side.
3. Let cool and slice into strips.
4. Combine all vinaigrette ingridients and toss with the cooked chicken. Add pasta and Mann's Power Blend. Top with sesame seeds.
5. Divide betweeen 4 containers and freeze.

Steak Marinade

Prep time: 2 minutes

Cooking time: 6 minutes

Servings: 4

Nutrients per serving:

Total Carbs – 6.3 g

Fat – 31.6 g

Protein – 32.8 g

Calories – 434

Ingredients:

- 4 steaks

Marinade:

- ½ cup olive oil
- 1/3 cup soy sauce
- 1/3 cup lemon juice
- ¼ cup Worcestershire sauce
- 3 Tbsp dried basil
- 1 1/2 Tbsp dried parsley
- 1 1/2 Tbsp garlic powder
- Pepper, to taste

Instructions:

1. Using a blender, combine all marinade ingridients.
2. Place the steaks into separate ziploc bags and add marinade.
3. Freeze.
4. When ready to cook, take the steak out of the freezer in advance and allow it to come down to room temperature. Place steak in a hot pan and cook for about 6 minutes, turning every minute.

Chicken Marinade

Prep time: 5 minutes

Cooking time: 1 hour

Servings: 4

Nutrients per serving:

Total Carbs – 6.2 g

Fat – 20.6 g

Protein – 41 g

Calories – 366

Ingredients:

- 2 lbs chicken thighs

Marinade:

- 1 cup plain yogurt
- 1 cup lemon juice
- 1 tsp curry powder
- 1 tsp tumeric
- 1 tsp cardamon
- Salt, to taste

Instructions:

1. Combine all marinade ingridients.
2. Marinate the chicken and cover with plastic wrap and freeze in the marinade.
3. When ready to cook, season with salt and place the chicken in a roasting pan. Bake at 375°F for about an hour until the chicken is golden.

Turkey Breast

Prep time: 15 minutes

Cooking time: 50 minutes

Servings: 6

Nutrients per serving:

Total Carbs – 6.2 g

Fat – 20.6 g

Protein – 41 g

Calories – 366

Ingredients:

- 3 lbs boneless, skinless turkey breast
- 2 sticks unsalted butter
- 2 Tbsp fresh sage, chopped
- 1 garlic clove, chopped
- 2 Tbsp chopped shallots
- Salt and pepper, to taste

Instructions:

1. In a skillet, brown 6 Tbsp butter. Add shallots, garlic, and sage, stir for one minute. Stir in the remaining butter and season with pepper and salt.
2. Coat the turkey with sage brown butter and place in a ziploc bag.
3. When ready to cook, wrap the turkey breast in foil and bake in the oven for 50 min at 350°F.

Dinner

Bean Casserole

Prep time: 10 minutes

Cooking time: 40 minutes

Servings: 6

Nutrients per serving:

Total Carbs – 26.6 g

Fat – 8 g

Protein – 11.7 g

Calories – 233

Ingredients:

- 2 cans (14 oz) white beans, rinsed
- 2 cans (14 oz) tomatoes, chopped
- 4 celery sticks, diced
- 4 carrots, diced
- 3 leeks,trimmed, sliced
- 2 garlic cloves, crushed
- 3 cups vegetable stock
- ½ cup white wine
- 3 Tbsp olive oil
- 1 handfull fresh oregano, chopped

Instructions:

1. In a large skillet, sauté celery and carrots in olive oil for 7 minutes.
2. Add the leeks, minced garlic, and wine. Cook until the liquid evaporates.
3. Add tomatoes and warm stock. Bring to boil, then let simmer for 35 minutes, stirring from time to time.
4. Stir in the beans and cook for 5 minutes.
5. Remove from heat and sprinkle with fresh oregano.
6. Freeze in plastic containers when cooled.

Tuna Noodle Caserole

Prep time: 20 minutes

Cooking time: 40 minutes

Servings: 4

Nutrients per serving:

Total Carbs – 25 g

Fat – 11 g

Protein – 19 g

Calories – 267

Ingredients:

- 12 oz egg noodle
- 12 oz can tuna, drained
- 1 1/2 cups milk
- 2 cans (10 oz) cream of mushroom soup
- Salt and pepper, to taste
- 1 cup grated cheese

Instructions:

1. Prepare noodles according to package directions.
2. In a separate bowl, mix soup & milk.
3. Add noodles and tuna. Season with salt and pepper.
4. Preheat oven to 350°F & grease a baking dish with cooking spray.
5. Bake for 30 minutes, then top with grated cheese and bake for 10 minutes more.
6. Freeze in foil or plastic containers.

Italian Sausage Casserole

Prep time: 20 minutes

Cooking time: 1 hour

Servings: 6

Nutrients per serving:

Total Carbs – 45 g

Fat – 8 g

Protein – 13 g

Calories – 310

Ingredients:

- 8 sweet Italian sausages, casings discarded
- 8 green onions, sliced
- 2 zucchini, diced
- 6 eggs
- 7 oz bell peppers, chopped, roasted
- 2 cups Cheddar cheese, shredded
- 1 1/2 cup milk
- 1 loaf Italian bread, cut into 1 inch cubes
- Salt and pepper, to taste

Instructions:

1. In a skillet, cook sausage until no longer pink.
2. Add onions and zucchini and sauté for 4 minutes.
3. Stir in roasted peppers. Season with salt and pepper.
4. Preheat the oven to 325°F.
5. Grease baking dish with cooking spray & add 4 cups bread cubes.
6. Top with half the sausages and half the cheese.
7. Add another layer of bread, then sausages, then cheese.
8. Whisk eggs with milk and pour over the cheese.
9. Bake covered for 1 hour.
10. Freeze in foil or plastic containers.

Mashed Potatoes Casserole

Prep time: 20 minutes

Cooking time: 45 minutes

Servings: 6

Nutrients per serving:

Total Carbs – 67 g

Fat – 5.7 g

Protein – 10.3 g

Calories – 357

Ingredients:

- 24 oz mashed potatoes
- 19 oz sweet ground turkey sausage, casings removed
- 2 cans diced tomatoes, with juice
- 1 onion, chopped
- ¼ cup fresh basil leaves, chopped
- 8 oz Italian Five Cheese Blend
- 1 tsp garlic and herb seasoning
- ¼ tsp Italian seasoning
- Salt and pepper, to taste

Instructions:

1. In a skillet, cook sausage until no longer pink.
2. Stir in onions and tomatoes and season with garlic and herb seasoning.
3. Preheat oven to 350°F.
4. Grease baking dish with cooking spray and transfer the sausages to the dish.
5. In a bowl mix together potatoes, cheese, and Italian seasoning.
6. Spread the potato mixture over the sausages.
7. Bake covered for 45 minutes.
8. Freeze in foil or plastic containers.

Crispy Casserole

Prep time: 20 minutes

Cooking time: 20 minutes

Servings: 6

Nutrients per serving:

Total Carbs – 17 g

Fat – 7.7 g

Protein – 7 g

Calories – 157

Ingredients:

- 2 cups cauliflower, chopped
- 2 cups broccoli, chopped
- 1 onion, chopped
- 1 cup milk
- 6 oz cream cheese, cubed
- 3 Tbsp butter
- 2 Tbsp flour
- 2 Tbsp Parmesn, grated
- 2/3 cup bread crumbs
- Salt and pepper, to taste

Instructions:

1. Place cauliflower and broccoli in a pot and add water to cover the vegetables.
2. Boil until the vegetables are tender.
3. Prepare a baking dish by greasing it with butter. Transfer cauliflower and broccoli to the dish.
4. In a skillet, sauté onion using 1 Tbsp butter until softened.

5. Add 1 Tbsp butter and stir until melted.
6. Season with salt and pepper. Add flour, constantly stirring.
7. Pour in milk. Cook, stirrring, for about 3 minutes, until bubbly.
8. Reduce heat and add cream cheese. Stir well.
9. Pour the milk mixture over the vegetables and bake at 350°F for 20 minutes.
10. Toss 1 Tbsp melted butter with bread crumbs and Parmesan. Sprinkle over the casserole.
11. Bake for 10 more minutes.
12. Serve cooled and freeze the leftovers.

Chicken Cordon Bleu Casserole

Prep time: 20 minutes

Cooking time: 35 minutes

Servings: 6

Nutrients per serving:

Total Carbs – 6 g

Fat – 6.3 g

Protein – 32 g

Calories – 219

Ingredients:

- 2 lbs skinless chicken breast, cooked, shredded
- ½ lb deli ham, sliced
- 1 can (10 oz) cream of mushroom soup
- 6 slices Swiss cheese
- ¾ cup milk
- ¼ cup mayonnaise
- 2 Tbsp butter, melted
- 2 tsp Dijon mustard
- ¼ cup bread crumbs
- Salt and pepper, to taste

Instructions:

1. Combine soup, mayo, and milk. Season with salt and pepper.
2. Divide the sauce between two bowls.
3. Coat the chicken with the sauce and transfer to a baking dish.
4. Sprinkle the ham over the chicken, and put the slices of Swiss cheese on top of ham. Pour the remaining sauce over the cheese.
5. In another bowl, mix the bread crumbs and butter, then sprinkle over the sauce.
6. Bake for 35 minutes at 350°F.
7. Serve and freeze the leftovers, covering with several layers of foil.

Lazy Casserole

Prep time: 20 minutes

Cooking time: 35 minutes

Servings: 6

Nutrients per serving:

Total Carbs – 2 g

Fat – 18 g

Protein – 17 g

Calories – 320

Ingredients:

- 1 head cabbage, shredded
- 1 onion, chopped
- 2 eggs
- 1 cup milk
- 2 sticks butter, melted
- 2 Tbsp olive oil
- 1 cup semolina
- Salt and pepper, to taste

Instructions:

1. In a bowl, combine milk and semolina.
2. In a skillet with some olive oil, sauté onions until translucent.
3. Add melted butter to milk-semolina mixture.
4. Add eggs to the mixture and stir. Season with salt and pepper.
5. Add onions and cabbage.
6. Grease a baking dish with butter. Pour the casserole mixture into the baking dish.
7. Bake for 30 minutes at 425°F.
8. Freeze in foil or plastic containers.

Tuna Casserole

Prep time: 20 minutes

Cooking time: 40 minutes

Servings: 6

Nutrients per serving:

Total Carbs – 30 g

Fat – 7 g

Protein – 16 g

Calories – 250

Ingredients:

- 16 oz elbow noodles, al dente, rinsed, drained
- 1 can (6.5 oz) tuna, shredded
- 1 batch simple white sauce (¼ cup flour
- ¼ cup butter, 2 cups chicken broth)
- 2 cups Cheddar cheese, shredded
- Salt and pepper, to taste (can add celery salt or onion salt as well)

Instructions:

1. Prepare simple white sauce by melting butter in a skillet and then stirring in flour, constantly whisking. Then add chicken broth and cook until bubbly.
2. Add half the tuna to the sauce.
3. In a large bowl, mix pasta, white sauce, the rest of the tuna, 1 cup cheese, and season with salt and pepper.
4. To freeze, cover with a foil before baking and put a label. When cooking let thaw, top with 1 cup Cheddar cheese, and bake at 350°F for 40 minutes.

Buckwheat Casserole

Prep time: 20 minutes

Cooking time: 40 minutes

Servings: 6

Nutrients per serving:

Total Carbs – 24.6 g

Fat – 14.4 g

Protein – 29 g

Calories – 340

Ingredients:

- 2 cups buckwheat, cooked
- 1 1/2 lbs ground chicken
- 2 onions, chopped
- 2 carrots, grated
- 2 apples, peeled, grated
- ½ cup hard cheese, grated

Instructions:

1. In a skillet, sauté onions and carrots using olive oil.
2. Combine ground chicken with onions and carrots. Season generously with salt and pepper.
3. Combine the cooked buckwheat with apples and cheese.
4. Prepare a baking dish by lining with parchment paper. Layer the chicken on the bottom, then buckwheat mixture.
5. Bake at 392°F for 30 minutes.
6. Take out and sprinkle with some more grated cheese and bake for 5 more minutes.
7. Freeze in foil or plastic containers.

Cream based Meat Casserole

Prep time: 15 minutes

Cooking time: 20 minutes

Servings: 6

Nutrients per serving:

Total Carbs – 18 g

Fat – 27 g

Protein – 23 g

Calories – 383

Ingredients:

- 1 lb ground meat (beef +pork)
- 2 eggs
- 2 Tbsp heavy cream
- 2-3 Tbsp oats, grinded
- Salt and pepper to taste
- Breadcrumbs for the dish bottom

Instructions:

1. Season ground meat with salt and pepper. Add oats and mix well.
2. Beat eggs together with cream. Add the cream mixture to the ground meat.
3. Put the mixture in a baking dish lined with breadcrumbs.
4. Bake at 392°F for 20-30 minutes.

Cabbage Casserole

Prep time: 30 minutes

Cooking time: 30 minutes

Servings: 4

Nutrients:

Sodium: 0.12 g

Potassium: 0.38 g

Total fat: 0.5 g

Calories: 93

Ingredients:

- ½ head white cabbage, shredded
- 2 eggs, beaten
- 2 Tbsp milk
- 2 Tbsp sour cream + more for serving
- 2 tsp semolina
- 1 dash salt
- Fresh parsley for garnish

Instructions:

1. In a saucepan, stew the shredded cabbage with milk until soft.
2. Sprinkle the semolina over the cabbage, constantly stirring, and cook for 10 minutes more.
3. Remove from heat, let cool & stir in the beaten eggs. Season with salt.
4. Arrange the cabbage mixture in a baking dish, coat with sour cream, and bake at 400°F for 20 minutes.
5. Serve with sour cream and fresh parsley.

Ground Meat Nests

Prep time: 20 minutes

Cooking time: 35 minutes

Servings: 6

Nutrients per serving:

Total Carbs – 12.6 g

Fat – 12.8 g

Protein – 16.3 g

Calories – 232

Ingredients:

- ½ lb ground meat (beef+pork)
- 1 raw egg
- 1 hard boiled egg, grated
- 1 onion, chopped, sautéed
- 1 potato, raw, grated
- ½ cup hard cheese, grated
- 2 tsp mayonnaise
- Salt and pepper, to taste

Instructions:

1. Season ground meat with salt and pepper. Mix together with raw egg.
2. On parchment paper, spoon the seasoned meat, forming "nests."
3. Spread some mayo over the nests and top with sauteed onions.
4. Add the grated potato, pepper, grated egg, salt and pepper, then cheese.
5. Preheat the oven to 356°F. Bake "nests" for 35 minutes.
6. Freeze in foil or plastic containers.

Moussaka

Prep time: 20 minutes

Cooking time: 35 minutes

Servings: 6

Nutrients per serving:

Total Carbs – 59 g

Fat – 18 g

Protein – 17 g

Calories – 470

Ingredients:

- 3 eggplants, sliced
- 2 squashes, sliced
- 2 tbsp Olive oil
- 17 oz potatoes, boiled in peel, half cooked
- 4 tomatoes, sliced
- 2 1/2 cups hard cheese, grated
- Fresh parsley for serving
- Salt and pepper, to taste

For the Béchamel sauce:
- 2 egg yolks
- 1 stick buttter
- 1 cup flour
- 1 1/2 cups milk
- Mediterranean herb blend

Instructions:

1. Season the eggplants and squash slices with salt and pepper. Sauté using olive oil.
2. Peel the cooled potatoes and cut into rounds.

3. Prepare the béchamel sauce: melt butter over low-medium heat, whisk in the flour. Add warmed milk and keep whisking.
4. Boil over low heat to thicken.
5. Remove from heat and stir in the egg yolks. Season with herb blend.
6. Line a baking dish with parchment paper.
7. Add one layer of sliced potatoes. Season with salt and pepper.
8. Top with cheese.
9. Add one layer of eggplant. Top with bechamel sauce.
10. Add layer of squash and top with the sauce.
11. Add a layer of tomatoes. Sprinkle with grated cheese.
12. Continue layering until out of ingredients.
13. Top with the remaining sauce and bake at 356°F for 30 minutes.
14. Sprinkle the moussaka with fresh parsley.
15. Freeze in foil or plastic containers.

Chicken Enchiladas

Prep time: 20 minutes

Cooking time: 30 minutes

Servings: 10

Nutrients per serving:

Total Carbs – 33 g

Fat – 5.6 g

Protein – 24 g

Calories – 286

Ingredients:

- 4 chicken breasts, boiled in salted water, shredded
- 1 onion, sliced
- 10 corn or flour tortillas
- 2 cans (14 oz) Red Enchilada Sauce
- 1 can (15 oz) black beans
- Jalapeño
- 3 cups Cheddar cheese, shredded

Instructions:

1. Mix shredded chicken, 1 can red enchilada sauce, onion, and half the cheese, beans, and jalapeño.
2. Fill each tortilla with chicken mixture. Roll it up & place in a baking dish.
3. Pour 1 can enchilada sauce over the tortillas.
4. Top with cheese.
5. Bake at 350°F for 30 minutes.
6. To freeze, cover with foil and label. When cooking, let thaw and bake at 350°F for 30 minutes.

Buttery Green Beans

Prep time: 10 minutes

Cooking time: 10 minutes

Servings: 4

Nutrients per serving:

Total Carbs – 8.9 g

Fat – 8.8.g

Protein – 2.3 g

Calories – 116

Ingredients:

- 1 lb green beans, trimmed
- 3 Tbsp butter
- 3 garlic cloves, minced
- 2 pinches lemon pepper
- Salt, to taste

Instructions:

1. In a pot, cover green beans with water. Bring to boil, then let simmer until soft.
2. Drain the water and add butter, cook, stirring for 3 minutes.
3. Stir in garlic and cook for 3-4 minutes. Season with lemon pepper and salt.
4. Freeze in plastic containers.

Dumplings Dough

Prep time: 20 minutes

Cooking time: 15 minutes

Servings: 4

Nutrients per serving:

Total Carbs – 286 g

Fat – 17.7 g

Protein – 42g

Calories – 1502

Ingredients:

- 1 egg
- 1 cup boiling water
- 1 Tbsp olive oil
- 3 cups flour
- Pinch of salt

Instructions:

1. Beat the egg and add salt.
2. Sieve flour and start kneading the dough. Add oil.
3. Add 1 cup boiling water.
4. Using hands, mix until not sticky to shape.
5. Roll out the dough into a thin layer. Cut out 3-inch rounds.
6. Fill each round to your liking (mashed potato/sauerkraut/cottage cheese). Fold in half and join the edges.
7. To cook, drop the dumplings into boiling water and cook for 10-15 minutes, stirring.
8. To freeze, place the dumplings on a sheet sprinkled with flour. Freeze until hard and then transfer to a bag with a label.
9. Cook frozen dumplings the same as fresh ones.

Chickpeas Pasta

Prep time: 10 minutes

Cooking time: 20 minutes

Servings: 4

Nutrients per serving:

Total Carbs – 63 g

Fat – 10 g

Protein – 26g

Calories – 434

Ingredients:

- 6 oz mushrooms, quartered
- 1 19-oz can chickpeas, drained
- ½ cup sun-dried tomatoes, chopped
- 2 cups dry pasta rotini
- 2 cups vegetable stock
- 3 cups spinach
- 1 cup Mozarella cheese, shredded
- Salt and pepper, to taste

Instructions:

1. Combine all ingridients exept stock in a container and freeze.
2. When ready to cook, in a pot, combine mushrooms, tomatoes, chickpeas, pasta, chicken stock,salt, and pepper.
3. Cover and bring to boil. Then let simmer for 10 minutes, stirring.
4. Stir in spinach and cheese and cook until the cheese is melted.

Recipe Index

CONCLUSION

Thank you for reading this book and having the patience to try the recipes.

I do hope that you gain as much enjoyment reading and experimenting with the meals as I have had writing this book.

If you would like to leave a comment, you can do it at the Order section->Digital orders, in your amazon account.

Stay safe and healthy!

Conversion Tables

VALUME EQUIVALENTS (LIQUID)

US STANDARD	US STANDARD (OUNCES)	METRIC (% PROXIMATE)
2 tablespoons	1 fl. oz.	30 mL
¼ cup	2 fl. oz.	60 mL
½ cup	4 fl. oz.	120 mL
1 cup	8 fl. oz.	240mL
1 ½ cup	12 fl. oz.	355 mL
2 cups or 1 pint	16 fl. oz.	475 mL
4 cups or 1 quart	32 fl. oz.	1 L
1 gallon	128 fl. oz.	4 L

OVEN TEMPERATURES

FAHRENHEIT(F)	CELSIUS(C) APPROXIMATE
250 °F	120 °C
300 °F	150 °C
325 °F	165 °C
350 °F	180 °C
375 °F	190°C
400 °F	200 °C
425 °F	220 °C
450 °F	230 °C

VALUME EQUIVALENTS (LIQUID)

US STANDARD	METRIC (APPROXIMATE)
$1/8$ teaspoon	0.5 mL
¼ teaspoon	1 mL
½ teaspoon	2 mL
$2/3$ teaspoon	4 mL
1 teaspoon	5 mL
1 tablespoon	15 mL
¼ cup	59 mL
$1/3$ cup	79 mL
½ cup	118 mL
$2/3$ cup	156 mL
¾ cup	177 mL
1 cup	235 mL
2 cups or 1 pint	475 mL
3 cups	700 mL
4 cups or 1 quart	1 L
½ gallon	2 L
1 gallon	4 L

WEIGHT EQUIVALENTS

US STANDARD	METRIC (APPROXIMATE)
½ ounce	15 g
1 ounces	30 g
2 ounces	60 g
4 ounces	115 g
8 ounces	225 g
12 ounces	340 g
16 ounce or 1 pound	455 g

Other Books by Emma Green

Intermittent Fasting https://goo.gl/i4WMva

South Beach Diet https://goo.gl/BKysXU

CPSIA information can be obtained
at www.ICGtesting.com
Printed in the USA
LVHW070909270920
667207LV00019B/3012